Business

Essential Tips on Ho

By: Michael Hendricks

9781635010442

PUBLISHERS NOTES

Disclaimer – Speedy Publishing LLC

This publication is intended to provide helpful and informative material. It is not intended to diagnose, treat, cure, or prevent any health problem or condition, nor is intended to replace the advice of a physician. No action should be taken solely on the contents of this book. Always consult your physician or qualified health-care professional on any matters regarding your health and before adopting any suggestions in this book or drawing inferences from it.

The author and publisher specifically disclaim all responsibility for any liability, loss or risk, personal or otherwise, which is incurred as a consequence, directly or indirectly, from the use or application of any contents of this book.

Any and all product names referenced within this book are the trademarks of their respective owners. None of these owners have sponsored, authorized, endorsed, or approved this book.

Always read all information provided by the manufacturers' product labels before using their products. The author and publisher are not responsible for claims made by manufacturers.

This book was originally printed before 2014. This is an adapted reprint by Speedy Publishing LLC with newly updated content designed to help readers with much more accurate and timely information and data.

Speedy Publishing LLC

40 E Main Street, Newark, Delaware, 19711

Contact Us: 1-888-248-4521

Website: http://www.speedypublishing.co

REPRINTED Paperback Edition: ISBN: 9781635010442

Manufactured in the United States of America

Dedication

This book is dedicated to every entrepreneur and aspiring entrepreneur. May this book give you full of helpful ideas to start and operate your business.

TABLE OF CONTENTS

Publishers Notes 2

Dedication 3

Chapter 1- Business Coaching for New Businesses 5

Chapter 2- Motivated Employees is Your Business' Success 16

Chapter 3- The Growth of Your Business 28

Chapter 4- Business Marketing Through Business Branding 42

Chapter 5- Business Operation 53

Chapter 6- Make Your Business Known 62

Chapter 7- Negotiation Mastery 78

About The Author 87

Chapter 1 - Business Coaching for New Businesses

The economy goes up and down. Right now, it's not doing so well. In fact, most would say it has tanked. Managing your costs is important to your growth and survival, and when the economy is performing poorly, it is even more of a challenge. Experts say that 58% of companies have a shortfall in leaders and many companies are actually cutting their development budget as part of their cost cutting measures.

Before you make that cut, you might want to think long and hard about whether that's the right choice for your business. When you take development away from the executives, it can be detrimental. Leading is actually special skill. A key leader can find a business coach a very helpful tool to navigate through the storm and continue to grow and prosper.

Business Ethics
Business Coaching and its Effects

Chances are more than 50% of your staff could benefit from business coaching and actually become motivated and energized again with a focus and a goal. Executive coaching involves working with the leaders of your company. These should be the people that are running in high gear. There are some key points where an executive coach can help leaders.

* Polish and fine tune their leadership skills

* Grow their leadership style

* Recalibrate what the success metrics look like

* Learn how to navigate through the times that are uncertain

* Lead teams with more motivation and power

The program that your business coach or executive coach puts together will be customized to the needs of your team and your leaders. Even leaders who are new to your team can find business coaching very beneficial.

The use of a business coach is still in its infancy. Businesses are often slow to make change, but those that are perceptive tend to think outside the box and use tools that can help them to make their business more successful. Business coaches and executive coaches can be beneficial to all sizes of business from the very small to the largest. They will benefit each business in their own unique way and that will depend on the current needs of the business are.

Whether it's a downturn in the economy or it's a struggle to get past a certain block; whether it's a desire to see your leaders think outside the box and grow or it's a desire to make sure that your staff are operating in their finest capacity; a business coach can help.

4 Reasons You Should Use a Business Coach to Get Results

Business coaching is a modern day concept. Many businesses, especially those that think outside the box, are recognizing that having a business coach is a powerful tool that your business can take advantage of. Let's look at 4 reasons you should use a business coach.

#1 A Business Coach Can Show You how to Get Greater Returns With Less Work

You work way too many hours and you believe if you were to leave even for a short vacation, things might fall apart, but boy, you are ready to work less! You can call the coaching by many names – executive coaching, small business coaching, business coaching and there are others

– bottom line is that any one of these can help your company to become far more efficient. That means you will work less hours and make more money. A business coach can help you turn your old business model into a new business model that's more powerful and profitable.

#2 Business Coaching Can Create More Profits

Are you ready to make more money? If you aren't making the profits you thought you would it's time to change that and turn things around. A business coach can help you do that. He or she

Business Ethics

can help you to jump start your business. Your business coach isn't there to make the decisions for you, but they are there to open you up and help you explore how you might reach the goals you have and make the profits you desire.

#3 Business Coaches Help You Develop Your Team

You are ready to build a team so that you can grow your business. That's great news. A business coach can help you recruit, train, and keep the right team members. When you build a team, it can motivate everyone and allow you to create a powerful team with the help of your business coach. You can create passion among your team members.

#4 Business Coaches Can Help You Find Your Passion

If you need to fall back in love with your business, a business coach is just the tool to help you do that. Overtime every business can become a bit mundane and a bit boring. Motivation is a key to maintaining and growing a vision and passion. Whether you are building a simple marketing plan or a full business your business coach is an excellent sounding board and can be an invaluable tool and sounding board to help you get your passion back!

A business coach is a service you have to pay for and that can sometimes stop people from making the call. Using a business coach is a great investment in your future.

Coaching to Get Results

Coaching has become a leading resource that business leaders are taking advantage of to create highly successful businesses. The one misunderstanding is that to use a business coach your business needs to be larger, but that's not the case at all.

Coaching can help create clarity and direction in any size business. Working with a business coach can help to determine what it is you want to create, the reason it is important, and how you plan to reach that goal. It can help you to create an action plan and then achieve the goals you set.

If you had an empowering way that you could commit to and then achieve your business goals, would you not want to take advantage of it? Well you do, it's called business coaching.

Business Coaching Helps You to Become Clear on Your Goals

It is important that you are clear on what it is you want from your business along with how you plan to get it. Then you will need to determine what your commitment is. A business coach can help you to create clear goals and plans on achieving those goals.

Business Coaching Aids You to be Effective and Productive

When it comes to support, business coaching provides individual attention along with the challenge and objectiveness that are needed. A skilled business coach is very successful because he or she can:

* Inspire you to expand your solutions

* Keep you focused on your goals

Business Ethics

* Make you accountable for your progress

* Support you through the change

* Remove any obstacles so that you can move forward

* Prioritize based on your values

* Challenges you to take the next step

Business Coaching Connects You to What's Important

Your business coach will help to build a foundation that's grounded so that you make decisions that are in alignment with your value system and what you value most. They will also help you to create a plan that will ensure your daily actions are in alignment with the values. This is the key to creating commitment breakthroughs.

A small business can benefit as much from a business coach as a larger business. Your business coach isn't there to make decisions for you, but rather to be a sounding board and to help guide you in the direction that is right for you and your business. Take advantage of outside help to grow your business.

How Business Coaching Helps Leadership Teams

Business coaching is an important tool that can offer a unique advantage if you want to coach your leadership teams, especially in a growing business. Business coaching can help to create an environment that is healthy for leadership growth that can play a key role as the business also grows.

It can help leaders to set strategic direction, develop marketing strategies and operating tactics in a low risk and non stressful manner that will improve the numbers and create a business that can run without being dependent on the owner or CEO.

The training manual used by the business coach should walk through the needs of the company. The business coach should also ensure that the members of the leadership team have their needs explored, their skills analyzed and their goals discussed. In that way, it's easier to make sure your leadership team members are strategically placed to maximize the benefits to the company and create the best environment for the leaders.

You should not confuse coaching with training, as they are different, especially when it comes to the delivery system. A coach will work with management to tailor a training program in the skill areas where there is a need for impact.

The coach will also help managers to make behavioral changes that are seen as necessary for growth. The significance is that the coach and the manager(s) must be clear on the competencies that will have an effect on the bottom line. It is essential that the competencies are measured before and after coaching so that there can be an evaluation of the effectiveness.

At the beginning the relationship is determined – is the coach considered a trusted friend or an advisor? Does the coach listen and provide feedback or does the coach help the manager obtain 360-degree feedback and then develop an action plan to increase performance? The role and the relationship need to be established by both parties before the coaching project begins.

The coach will push the window with each manager to help them grow professionally and to promote the company's success and the success of the leadership team. A good way to do this is to create a situation so that each leadership team member will ask for help

Business Ethics

from the coach, rather than the coach forcing their help on the manager.

Business coaching doesn't look just one way. It is designed to be created to work specific to the needs of the client and in doing so the delivery can be tailor made.

How Business Coaching Works

We hear a lot about business coaching these days, but you may not actually understand how it works and what it's really all about. In fact, you may have considered business coaching, but then changed your mind because you weren't really sure your company needed it.

Business coaching will apply the essential coaching principles to every part of a business or organization. It will follow meticulous and detailed methodology to ensure both facilitative coaching processes and management consulting tools are employed and put into place in the manner they should be.

It is acknowledged just how important the role of employee productivity is to any business or organization. Therefore, it is also interesting and important to know about the productivity components and their role in the business success.

Employees at every level of the organization must have the proper skill and the skills they have must be properly used. Employees need to be motivated in order for optimal productivity to occur and for the corporations or organizations' vision to be fulfilled.

The matching of skill and experience of employees to positions within the company or organization is generally managed through the HR department that is responsible for creating the HR processes including recruitment and training. Management teams usually manage the planning and use of staff to get the highest production. However, few companies actually manage employee motivation very well. It is rarely recognized or understood. Recent motivational studies that have been done by Harvard research confirm this.

Motivating your employees by throwing incentives at them, can work for a short time; however, if you want sustainable motivation there must be an alignment between the employee's personal goals and aspirations and the company's needs. This alignment is what the business coaching process can do for a business or organization and it is also where the success lies.

The Business Coaching Process

There is really no such thing as a generic business coaching process. Solutions should be catered to each businesses needs. The process will look much different for a company that is restructuring one department than a company that is undertaking a cultural shift throughout the organization.

Business coaching is a powerful tool that can transform a business form just surviving to highly successful. It can help to change the way processes flow within an organization or create an entirely new workplace environment. Business coaching is limited only by your needs and your budget. There are few companies that can't benefit from an outsiders viewpoint and skills.

Business Ethics

Business coaching can be a valuable investment.

Highly Effective Business Coaching

Business coaching — what is it? Executives and managers of companies who are interested in development and career growth increasingly turn to a business coach to have a customized development process. Consider this — how often would you have found it helpful to have a chance to talk about some key ideas with a person that is impartial and objective in preparation for a major change or perhaps a very important meeting.

The concept of business coaching has actually come from the sports arena where top athletes employ coaches to help improve and enhance their performance. Business people are slowly realizing that the same benefits can be enjoyed in the business arena using business coaches.

Coaching works best in those environments where there is a desire to be practical, progressive and proactive but at the same time there is value in the opportunity to challenge and stimulate. The executive(s) or manager(s) is thought to be the expert in his/her field and in this way the business coach will facilitated the executive or manager to find the right way forward. Coaching is always forward thinking with a well-structured approach that remains flexible and presumes purpose and commitment.

Effective, Efficient, Productive

When it comes to professional support, business coaching is the exception as it combines individual attention, challenge and objectiveness. The coach's skills make it extremely successful because:

It inspires you to develop your own solutions

It keeps you focusing on a specific goal or goals It makes you accountable for your progress

It supports you through change

It removes any blockages so that you can move forward It prioritizes based on values

It challenges you to take the next step in moving forward

Research published in Olivero et al. 1997 showed that training can increase productivity by as much as 22 percent, but when training is combined with coaching, it can increase productivity by a whopping 88 percent.

What Does Business Coaching Involve?

Coaching is not training – the delivery system is much different. A business coach will work with the executive or manager to develop a training program that is tailored to the skill areas where there is a need for impact. The coach will help the executive/manager to make the necessary behavioral changes to create growth. The coach does not provide the answer, but rather the coach brings along a process or system to help the client determine the answers.

Chapter 2 - Motivated Employees is Your Business' Success

Those companies that are highly effective take great pains to make sure that they have established a clear vision for their company along with a clear and concise strategy of how they want to implement that vision.

They carefully recruit and retain those employees who are the best to help them carry out their strategy. After all, it is common sense that if you want your company to have a high degree of success you need to have high and continuous employee production, because you can't do it alone. This means you also have continually motivated employees.

Michael Hendricks

By definition, employee motivation is a key component of the employee productivity equation. It is in this area where you will find that business coaching can have the biggest impact. You can temporarily boost your employees' motivation using incentives, especially financial incentives, but these are not sustainable employee motivation methods and they will stop working.

Business coaching can help you to create sustainable employee motivation.

A company establishes its vision, mission and execution strategy. An employee also needs to establish their own vision. It will just be minus all the corporate 'talk,' and it will be their terms, what they want out of their career at the company.

A business coach will support employees using a mix of individual sessions and group sessions. They will help employees to articulate what it is they want, their goals, and then help them to determine how they might reach those goals in relation to the company they work for.

Employees usually find these types of sessions far more useful than when companies use 'Personal Development Plan' templates. Actually, when the results are structured right, they can actually take the templates and transfer them to work effectively for personal development.

Facilitative coaching sessions will take a bottom up data approach that details the skills of each employee and what their motivators are to reconcile with the objectives of the business. The focus is to align corporate objectives to the needs of the employees.

Of course, not all employees will get what it is they want. It will be up to your management team to negotiate a solution that is a win-

Business Ethics

win for everyone involved. Management will also have to effectively create the basis for the sustainable employee motivation to get the most out of the process.

A Look at the Different Coaching Styles

Many people are unaware that there are a number of different coaching styles that can be used by a coach. Let's have a look at some of these different coaching styles.

* Traditional Coaching Model — The coach identifies with how the client is feeling. The coach acts as a guide and confidant.

* Advanced Coaching Model — Useful when there is a need to make a considerable break from the past, and where the person wants to try new things or a new way of doing something.

* Block Removal Coaching — This coaching model works when a person is resistant to growth, which causes a block, that usually the result of a hidden fear or limiting beliefs.

* Innovation Coaching Model — This coaching model focuses on experimentation, creativity and innovation.

* 3-D Coaching Model — This coaching model works on who a person is and what they want, then how to get it.

* Personal Foundation Model — The coach will work on standards and boundaries. The higher a person wants to go, the deeper the foundation has to be.

* Bigger Thinking Model — The coach will challenge the person's assumptions and work to break one out of their comfort zone and expand their thinking!

* Solution Coaching — The coach will identify symptoms, find out the source of those symptoms, and then work with a person to find a solution.

* Shift Coaching Model — When a person isn't able to determine how to achieve their goals, a shift in thinking can help. The coach can help a person to step back, shift, and then move forward.

* Deep Coaching — There can be a shift in basic beliefs over time until these beliefs simply are not true any longer. The coach can help a person dig deep to discover the 'out of date truth' which a person can then align with the reality of today.

* Performance Coaching Model — For the client that is competitive, the coach can help by developing a persuasive goal, creating milestones to help you focus on your goals, and building momentum through reporting daily.

* Acceptance Coaching Model — Rather than a person trying to overcome a weakness, the coach can help to accept it and use it to their advantage.

* Intermediate Model — A good model when a person wants the coach to work in partnership on developing goals and then on achieving them.

As you can see, there are many different ways that business coaching can be approached. It can pay to match the coach's style with your needs to get the best results. Talk to the coach you are considering hiring and see what style they use. Don't be afraid to ask questions so you make the right choice.

Business Ethics
Coaching Models for the Workplace

The earliest coaching models date back the 1950s and through the 1980s, they were still static models. It wasn't until the 1990s, when sports coaching models began to grow in popularity. A coaching model needs to be flexible and adaptable so that it can be tailored to the specific needs of the client. Today's coaching model should:

* Presents a complete, detailed description of the process that's involved

* It should build towards an outcome that's predicted

* It should establish the nature of the components

* It uses valid methodology to produce change that is sustainable and measurable

The traditional coaching model was built around change models that were outdated like the grow model, action planning, goal setting, etc. fall very short of creating lasting behavior competencies that are measurable. Using a 'one size fits all' approach is simplistic and ineffective because it ignores the person's behavioral pattern that controls how the skill that's going to be improved is executed.

With traditional coaching very shortly after those who participated revert back to their old behaviors after the event. It seems it's a pretty expensive venture for a quick buzz that fades fast. The challenge for development professionals is to improve the organization's effectiveness through behavioral change that involves a learning model that strengthens the individuals and sustains the behavioral skills.

Michael Hendricks

The 21st century professional coaching is a combined approach that the behavioral sciences founded. Today's coaching model includes personal beliefs, development, attitudes, values, motivation, social learning and emotions along with organizational and personal dynamics.

Many mechanisms of the behavioral based coaching model come from the behavioral approach to learning and changing. Some of the coaching model aspects are:

* Targeting and then focusing on an explicit behavior

* Analyzing a behavior in relation to its precursor and the consequences

* Applying a reliable and valid method of data collection, data analysis and assessment

* Building of a developmental plan

* Employing behavioral change techniques that are validated

* Measuring, managing and maintaining behavioral change

Coaching models for the workplace need to be effective long term. They shouldn't provide the answers, but rather the circumstances for the participant(s) to come up with their own solutions that will work.

The coach is a bit like a sounding board opening up a dialogue that will help the participants to grow and prosper and that can help a business to grow and prosper as well.

Business Ethics
How One on One Business Coaching Can Help

Business coaches can be a powerful tool for any business environment. They can help business managers in innovative companies to understand and take the next step in solving a specific technology or business development. A business coach can help your company reach the next stage in product development.

When business coaching is done on a one on one basis it can be offered in many forms such as weekly or monthly and each session can last from a couple of hours to a full day. Monthly programs tend to work well with small to mid size businesses where there is only one owner or one partner. The company's commitment to business coaching should be long term. On average 9 to 12 months is the commitment period. Most business coaches can create custom packages for you.

ROI for the Business Owner

Using the unique approach of having a business coach work with your management team or other employees, can be highly beneficial to your ROI. The increase in profitability using a business coach is well documented.

Business coaching can result in a larger market share, improved talent retention, lower operating costs, improved marketing, faster methods to get the product to market, greater customer satisfaction and overall streamlining. The use of personal that's from outside the organization can help you to see things differently and help you to grow and prosper.

You Have the Choice

The business coaches one of the most powerful word is 'choice.' A person can choose to make change, to grow, to learn, to evolve. In fact, no matter what your choice is, change is going to occur. The change will bring about a new environment and it can reunite your passion and change your perception, which becomes your reality. Innovative leadership is a powerful tool for any business.

Business coaching does a great job of increasing self awareness, and helping a business owner see how they are being perceived and then redefine that perception.

A business coach can help you to identify the core strengths and core behaviors of the management and leadership team to ensure all involved clearly understand how to select and optimize the most powerful asset any business has – that is the human potential. The reality is the success or failure of any business comes down to the humans that are involved and the decisions that are made.

Coaching allows you to look at old habits and then choose new ones that are more powerful strategies.

The One on One Coaching Model

The one on one coaching model is an excellent choice if you want to invest in the talent for the future. It can play a positive role in the long-term strategy and yet often it is a strategy that's overlooked.

The coaching relationship is going to enhance the skills that are needed during difficult and changing times. When your company invests in this type of development of company talent, they are looking at a long-term strategy for their company and one that can

Business Ethics

be created using the one on one coaching model. It looks similar to this.

* The coach will meet with the manager(s) and Human Resource Dept. to talk about the goals of the candidate and they will come to an agreement on the targets.

* The coach will meet with the candidate to collect personal history, career data and then to reach an agreement on the goals and expectations.

* The assessment process will begin by using a variety of instruments along with the 360 feedback from employees that work in close proximity with the candidate.

* Feedback is collected and then it is analyzed to decide on assets and liabilities, which are then presented to the candidate.

* The candidate will create a developmental plan that's specific to behavior and determine the desired outcome that will also include input from the manager and/or Human Resources personal.

* The plan is implemented so that it also has time frames and suitable tools.

* The coach works with the candidate to incorporate the new behaviors with the regular one-on- one session.

* The coach will reassess the close-working employees, and then evaluate and report the incremental shifts. Engagement will extend when there is a revised objective.

Choosing a Coach

Choosing the right coach is important. It means you need to find out who best fits the candidate. Personalities vary, but still professionals should be able to blend with a mix of personalities. A professional coach should have these qualifications:

* Experience in the industry.

* Exposure to working with senior staff and the types of issues they face.

* Exposure to and/or certification in numerous assessment tools.

* Being able to provide feedback.

* Five or more years of corporate coaching are preferred.

* Expertise and significant exposure in organizational changes.

You've heard it before – when the going gets tough the tough get going, or they should take advantage of one on one coaching to help create opportunities and make goals. A coach is able to reinforce the needed skills for both current personal and new personnel so that they can move forward.

The Role of the Business Coach Put into Play

The concept of business coaching actually got its start on the sports field. In sports, top athletes have coaches to help improve their performance and enhance their abilities. That concept has been transposed to the players in the business arena who have realized that the same methodology can apply in the business environment.

Business Ethics

Executives and managers can improve their performance and enhance their skills by having a business coach.

Initially a meeting needs to be established with the business coach who will assist in identifying the requirements so that a specific program can be created to meet those requirements.

Coaching can also be extended out to employee groups or kept at the individual level. The business coach isn't there to bring the answers. Their role is to bring a process or a system that will help the client to discover their own answers.

Accepted as a Coach

An effective coach will define the relationship right at the beginning. The role could be that of a trusted advisor or friend, it could as a sounding board and to provide feedback, it could be as a performer to help create a plan. This needs to be established early and this role must accepted by both parties if it's going to work.

The coach will push the envelope with each manager he/she works with so that they can grow professionally and play a major role in both the company's success and their individual success.

The Coach Isn't the One in Control

It is important to remember that the coach is a resource and he/she is not in control of the relationship, the decisions or the actions of the person being coached. Sometimes the coach does form a partnership with the coached manager that helps develop good decisions and choices for the company and the manager's personal growth.

Michael Hendricks

However, ultimately the manager will make the final decisions, not the coach. Your effectiveness as a communicator and your knowledge along with the relationship you have developed will ultimately play a role in whether a manager chooses to incorporate any recommendations you might have.

The role of the coach should be clear. As important as the coach can be to a company and the management and staff, they are the out-sider looking in and it is very important that clear and concise guidelines are established from the very beginning to make sure that no lines are crossed.

Chapter 3 - The Growth of Your Business

Your business is doing okay, but you'd like to see it grow and prosper. That doesn't seem to be happening. If you are wondering what you should do, it's a place many business owners find themselves. A good place to start is with a business coach, who can help you to grow your business.

A Business Coach Helps You to Navigate Market and Economic Changes

You are very aware that you need to grow your business, but for that to happen and for you to grow you will have to learn more. It's hard keeping up with changes in the industry, never mind the changes that occurring on a global business scale. Trying to figure out how to improve your role in the mix can be a bit daunting. Business education is now in a new realm with business coaching and business mentoring replacing the more traditional form of consulting, seminars and books. So if you want to get it right it's time to turn to your business coach.

Business Coaches Can Establish Accountability

Your business coach is going to hold you accountable, to demand you see results and to demand you see a profit. Your business coach is someone who can push you, challenge you, encourage you to think outside the box, and congratulate you when you succeed. It can be a lonely job being the owner and you often don't have the sounding board that you desire or need. A trained business coach can help you to solve the problems that arise and to turn these situations into opportunities.

Business Coaches Can Offer You a Second Opinion From Another Expert

You need a business coach to demand results and hold you accountable. You need a business coach who can see through the maze and who isn't blinded by the industry or that fact that there is too much competition. You want a business coach who can keep his or her eye on the prize. That's a powerful combination for you.

Like your life, running your business can be challenging and there can certainly be ups and down. Sometimes it's the simplest of things that hang you up and you can't work your way through it. A business coach cannot only offer you a second opinion, they can be a great sounding board to help you get over your stumbling block.

Why not join the thousands of small businesses that are turning to business coaches for help growing their business.

Business Ethics
Training Methods and Techniques Used By Business Coaches

In order for a business to transform into a great business, it will have to recognize the strengths of the people that work for the company. Bottom line – your company is only as good as the people you have working for you. If you want to unleash the full power of your company, it will have to begin with the individual.

When the individuals, employees are shown how to self manage and to upgrade their professional skill set as well as their personal skill set; and when they learn how to feel alert, balanced, powerful and in control; it is then that they will have the largest contribution to your company. When your company is able to move its people into an optimum zone, with sustainable top performance, the company will also have top performance.

There are many different training techniques and methods that can be used. The focus is on developing further the employee's thinking skill set and to give them the edge. Here are just a few tips and tricks to consider incorporating into the training.

Make sure that the training techniques and methods

* Will improve the employee's overall well-being. This includes immediate performance and long-term.

* Are filled with fast paced learning that's fun and relevant to 'real life' experiences and that everyone can immediately.

* Will provide positive changes in the thinking skills of employees that affect their professional skills.

* Are loyal to the employers and build exceptional goodwill throughout the organization.

* Integrates well with other development and training initiatives.

* This will cost significantly less than other comparable development and training solutions.

Benefits to the Workplace

* An increase in productivity

* Challenges you to take the next step

* Learning to maximize the workload in the workplace

* Minimize the stress in the workplace

* Help to find focus and build self confidence

* Prioritize based on your values

* Improved career direction

* Employees experience more fulfillments

* Employee enlightenment

* Inspire you to expand your solutions

* Remove any obstacles so that you can move forward

* Keep you focused on your goals

* Make you accountable for your progress

* Support you through the change

Business Ethics

There are numerous training methods and techniques used by business coaches in the workplace. No one method is right or wrong, but it is helpful when the business coaches are able to cater their training methods to the environment.

Understanding the Role of the Business Coach

The business coach is an important asset that savvy businesses and organizations are taking advantage of their services. Still, many don't fully understand the role of the business coach in today's modern business, so let's have a look.

#1 A Business Coach Supports the Employee

It's usually executives or managers that seek guidance or input from a coach when they are not sure how to handle a certain situation.

Sometimes help is sought before a tentative or difficult situation is dealt with. Managers will often seek assistance with their own growth as a manager, which can leave coaches with a very difficult and delicate situation.

A coach has the ability to improve the executive's abilities and self esteem, especially if there is confirmation that his or her answer is right. If a coach doesn't know what the right answer or is speculating the correct course of action is the truth. It's far better to say you do not know than to give bad advice.

#2 A Business Coach Helps Manager to Develop Their Solutions

People usually know how to act or what they should do. Many time's the job of the coach is to draw out the answer from the person, because if you give him/her the answer then they are less likely to own the solution. A coach can offer options and make resource recommendations, even give opinions. A coach can answer questions, but in the end the manager must have the answer.

#3 A Coach Must Have Communication Skills That Are Sharpened

Listening is a key skill all coaches need to have in order to be able to understand the actual needs of the manager who is asking for their assistance.

It is a coach weakness when he or she assumes the current situation or question is like one previously encountered. The coach needs to be fully engaged and aware to take in the information that is being provided. Open ended questions are necessary to draw out the manager. Listening includes watching body language, facial expression, tone of voice, and movements.

#4 A Coach is a Teacher or Educator

As an external coach you teach managers and leaders as you work with them. The goal is to make them self sufficient. The role of the coach is to provide them with the tools they need to be successful in their business arena.

What is Business Coaching and How Can it Benefit Your Business

Business coaching – you may have heard a lot of buzz around it, but might still not be sure exactly what it is. A business coach is like a mentor that can help you and your business. Your focus and your goal are to grow your business, increase your profits and be highly successful.

Business Ethics

You might have lots of ideas on how to take your business to the next level, but wouldn't it be helpful if you had someone you could bounce those ideas of that was objective and impartial?

Wouldn't it be beneficial to have someone to talk to about key ideas to make major changes to your business? That's where a business coach can help. They aren't there to give you the answers. They are there to help you work through your ideas and answers to find clarity and move forward.

Business coaching is most effective when those involved want to be practical and progressive while at the same time being proactive rather than reactive.

A business coach will be most effective those who like to be stimulated and challenged. As a business owner, this likely describes you and so you can see why the use of a business coach could be highly beneficial to you and your company. Business coaching is structured forward thinking that is also flexible with commitment and purpose.

Business coaching is so successful because it:

* Will motivate you to create solutions

* Will help you to focus on your specific goals

* Will make you accountable for the progress you do or do not make

* Will support you through the transition

* Will remove any stumbling blocks so you can move forward

* Will help you to prioritize

* Will challenge you to move forward

Do not confuse training with coaching. The way it is delivered is significantly different. A business coach will work with you to create a training program for your company.

That training program will be tailored to meet the needs of your business. The skills that are needed to grow your business will be addressed. Your business coach will make changes to help take your business to the next step. The coach doesn't have the answers, you do and he or she will help you to bring those ideas to life. Now that you know exactly what a business coach is, the time might be now to use their services.

Using Reflective Language in Business Coaching

Business coaching is a powerful tool, and it becomes even more useful when reflective language is used, which is the reflecting back of what the coach says in his or her own words. This leads to a win-win situation, ideal for success.

With reflective language, the coach isn't using mental activity to interpret and there is no need for the coach to become detached from their experience because they are worried about the meaning of the coach's words. The best coaches use reflective language and while the coaches might not notice when reflective language is used, those observing most certainly do.

The reflective language is intended to help the employees stay connected to their discovery process. The words expressed are then reflected back in as perfect a form as possible so that there is no need to translate them.

Business Ethics

Words are let out and then reflected right back, without any resistance. The coach never once questions the words because the words are theirs. The process of reflective questioning is so perfect that the employee doesn't even notice the sentence construction and they are able to stay focused on their own thinking and discovery evolution.

Sub Modalities

Sub modalities a just experience variants. In coaching, there is the possibility of extending the employee's experiences in the world by inviting the audience to focus on their experiences and then play them. This isn't a new concept dating back to the 1960s, but it still remains important today. When you explore the sub modalities of experiences it can lead to a change in visual and auditory representation.

When you watch a person's language, you will get clues on how they store information. Inviting an employee to experiment with sub modalities of their experience can help them to find ways that are more constructive to manage situations in the future and it can provide a routine support system for those tough scenarios.

Sub modalities can be a bit hard to understand, but there is a great deal of information available online that will help you to better understand. You will even be able to find some working examples.

Reflective language is a powerful tool that business coaches can use when working with employees. It's a tool that is often overlooked and yet has so much value. Business coaching is a powerful tool that most companies can really benefit from.

Michael Hendricks
What is Business Coaching and What Can it Do for You

Coaching is a process that enables executives, managers and staff to achieve their full potential. Coaching and mentoring are similar in nature. Let's look at some of the things your business coach will do for you, your staff and your business.

* Will teach clients to creatively apply techniques and tools. This includes things like facilitating, doing one-on-one training, counseling and networking.

* Encourages clients to a commitment to action and the development of growth and change that's lasting.

* Encouraging clients to constantly advance competencies and to expand developmental association whenever necessary to attain their goals.

* Ensure that clients build their personal competencies and that they don't build unhealthy dependencies on the coaching relationship.

* Evaluate the outcome of the process, with the use of objective measures when possible to make sure the relationship thrives and the client is achieving their goals both personal and work related.

* Facilitate the exploration of the client's needs, desires, motivations, skills and the thought process to assist the client in making real and lasting changes.

* Preserve positive unconditional regard for the client, which means that the coach is always non judgmental and supportive of the client, their aspirations and views.

Business Ethics

* Management of the relationship to make sure the client get a suitable level of service and that the program isn't too long or too short.

* Observe the client, listen and ask questions to understand the situation of the client.

* Use questioning techniques to make possible the client's own thought processes to identify solutions and actions rather than using a direct approach.

* Proven coaching training practices can bolster trust, strengthen relationships and commitment, and enjoy the benefits of open communication.

* Give meaningful feedback to clients on the best way to communicate requests and suggestions to others?

* Provide skill to build trust and acceptance.

* Teach clients how to use questions to achieve the best performance.

* Examine the behaviors that will lead to unreliable behavior and the inability to achieve the client's goals.

Business coaching is a valuable tool where a trained professional comes into a business no matter what the business size to work with executives, managers, and staff so that they can create their goals and achieve those goals, so that they can grow and expand their skills and improve their role in the workplace achieving their goals.

Michael Hendricks
Why Using a Business Coach Can Get You the Results You Want

The modern day business looks much different than it did a few decades ago and business coaching is a relatively new concept too. It's been proven to be highly valuable and effective, which is why so many businesses today find business coaches a powerful tool that can help grow their business. Businesses that are more forward thinking are quick to recognize the benefits of using a business coach.

Businesses want to grow their profits. After all, that's what business is about right. If you are ready to see your bottom line grow and you aren't satisfied with your current bottom line, you might consider using a business coach who can aid in giving your business a boost. Your business coach isn't there to make decisions for you. Instead the role of the business coach is to help you open up and to aid you in exploring how you can reach your goals and make the profit you desire.

Using a business coach can help you to discover how you can work less and make more. There's this mistaken identity with the harder you work the better. But actually most people work too many hours, don't take enough vacations and don't get the rest they need. Things can start to fall apart if you aren't taking care of yourself. A business coach can help you discover how you can work less and make more, turning over a new leaf from your old business model to a new business model that's more profitable.

A business coach can help you to develop your team and grow your business, helping you to train and recruit the right members for your team. Building a strong team is a good way to motivate everyone in the team and it allows for the creation of a very powerful team that's passionate.

Business Ethics

It's pretty common for a person to lose their passion over time. The same applies to you and your business. Whether it's you as the business own that's lost your passion or your staff that boredom and mundane behavior can jeopardize the success and growth of any business.

Motivation is behind every passion and every vision. Your business coach can help motivate you and/or staff again by becoming the sounding board for new ideas. Bring the passion into your business and watch it grow.

Why You Want to Hire the Services of a Business Coach

You are ready to take your business to the next level. Sure, it's healthy, but you also realize that without growth that it will stagnate and could also become nonviable. Yet, so far you just can't seem to make it happen. You just haven't been able to take it to the next level. The time is now – hire a business coach to help you expand and grow your business.

We are all familiar with sports coaches. They help athletes to perform their best. Well a business coach is the equivalent in the business world. A business coach can help you navigate through the ups and downs of a changing economy and a changing market. May times the missing component to a growing business is knowledge. As you learn more about your industry, the global market and your role in the mix you will be able to make sound decisions on your growth.

A business coach can help you to do that through business education, which is accomplished through business coaching and replacing a more conventional method of learning that involves seminars, books and consulting. If you want to get the advantage over the competition turn to a business coach.

Your business coach isn't going to create solutions for you. They are going to be a sounding board for you and they are going to hold you accountable for results.

Expect your business coach to push you, encourage you and challenge you to open up your thinking to look outside the box and most importantly to succeed. As an owner, you already know it's lonely at the top and many times you don't have anyone to bounce ideas off or talk through those ideas.

A business coach can be that person. They can also help you problem solve and turn problems into opportunities.

Having a business coach working with you gives you a chance for a second option from another highly respected professional. Your business coach should help you navigate the maze and when you hire a business coach, they can help you to keep your focus on the reward at the end of the tunnel – the increased profits.

You're a business owner and that can be challenging. Every business has its good times and low times. Sometimes the problem is an easy fix other times it requires more in-depth thinking and it can be what holds your business back. Having a business coach can be just what you need to remove the obstacle and see clearly what needs to occur for you to move forward, grow your business and increase your profits.

Chapter 4 - Business Marketing Through Business Branding

Branding is all about image of a business. The concept doesn't only include style, emblems and logos but also the image of quality perceived. The image perceived may be of total quality, reliability, and more.

Branding is about the business and how a business is different from the competitors. The purpose of a brand is to distinguish yourself from your competitors. Once you make a distinguishing impact then an advertising campaign can be much more effective.

The success of a company can be determined by a brand. Branding includes many factors which help a company be successful. these factors may include a website, marketing efforts, and anything that gives a company an identity. Consumers trust wholeheartedly a corporate image because there is a psychology in motivating the purchasing decisions.

All companies should practice branding. Brick and mortar business and online companies benefit through branding methods. It is common for smaller companies and online businesses to fail due to a lack of understanding about the importance and factors of a good brand.

Branding ensures professionalism with a company. It seals the deal on an entire package. A small company with a brand looks just as good as a large corporation when they practice the right techniques. Brands enhance your confidence as a business owner but also in the consumers that you really can deliver what you promise.

Branding offers consistency with a business. It gives direction to employees and customers know what to expect. Consistency can be performed through the use of things like business cards, t-shirts, and more. Consistency includes visibility techniques that are professional and will remain in the memory of a consumer.

One concept that consumers often attach to a brand is called brand equity. A brand is often considered to be an asset also. For example, if you have developed a very good brand that is well known as being a top distributor of massage chairs and you have a competitor with a brand known to provide defective products, your brand will be worth more.

Business Ethics
What you Need About Branding

Branding is all about what the customers perceive of your company. Your brand is the promise that you intend to make to the customers. The ultimate goal is to spark an emotional connection in order to create a positive feeling resulting of loyalty to a specific product from the customers.

Most customers hold true to products they enjoy. It is very common for a customer to be impressed with a brand and continue to buy a product based on that brand. You want to create these feelings of loyalty to bring the customers back for more. This is the ultimate goal.

Mission and Vision of Your Company

The mission and vision of your company should uphold excellence in providing a quality product to customers that you care about. These are statements about your company regarding the ultimate goals you wish to achieve within your endeavors. Many companies focus their vision or mission on their employees while others extend their mission outward to the customers. There should be a fine mix here with both.

Many customers do not read into a vision or mission statement too often. However, that doesn't mean that you shouldn't take it seriously. Your vision and mission are both a part of the branding process because they define what your company is all about. These two statements need to be believed and practiced by employees and all staff of the company.

Benefits and Features of Your Products or Services

A big part of creating a brand for your business is proving to the customers why your products and services are the best to buy. Differentiation takes place here but you need to prove the benefits to the consumers. Determine what the benefits are with the products you offer, the services you offer, or something else. Why does the customer benefit when they shop or buy from you? You will have a very hard time establishing a brand if you cannot determine the benefits or your products or services.

The features of your products and services are also important and they go hand in hand with the benefits. The features of a specific product should provide a benefit. Determine the features and the ones that stand out from the rest or provide the biggest benefit may be a target for the marketing campaign.

Customers Perception Today

Branding is about customer's perception. When you want to create a brand you want to create a perception of the customer that you are the best, provide quality, or maybe even more.

It is important to have a good idea of what the customers currently think of you when you are building a branding campaign. Today customers may not know that you exist or they may have a negative feel for your business because you haven't been practicing proper methods. Have a clear understanding on exactly what the customers think of you.

If you are unsure what the customers think of you then you may need to send out surveys and questionnaires. These types of things can help you get a good idea where you stand with the perception

Business Ethics

of the customers. It is okay if it is bad today. It will give you something to build on with your branding campaign.

Qualities Perceived by the Customers

The next thing you need to do with a branding campaign is to determine the different qualities that are perceived about your products by the customers. Do you have a good reputation with the consumer world for providing total quality in your products or are your products considered to be garbage and not worth the money?

The qualities of your business may be many things. When you think about how customers consider the qualities of your business, make sure you consider the products you offer, the customer support you provide, your image, or anything else that would make a customer think of quality coming from your company.

The vision and mission statement are very important for every business no matter how big or small. Make sure that your brand works well and matches what you say you want to deliver. Determine what the benefits and features of your business are and have a clear picture on this. You will need this information to provide a clear picture when you focus on developing your brand.

Also learn about what the customers really think of you. You might think customers absolutely love you when they are really bashing you on the quality of your product. Knowing what the customers think is very important. Creating a brand based on customer input can be successful, especially if you change the design of something for the customers. This gives them a sense of ownership and it shows them you really do care.

Your Target Market

Audience is everything. If you do not know the audience that you are targeting then you cannot begin creating a brand for a product or a company. There are many reasons that audience must be considered. Knowing your audience well will work for you in the long run.

The audience is the targeted customer base that you are hoping to reach out to for purchasing your product. Audience may include gender, age, geographical regions, and more.

The age of an audience must be considered when branding occurs. This is because if you are targeting a younger and more hip crowd they may want to see a brand that is vibrant and more hip. If your audience is older and more sophisticated then they may be looking for a brand displaying more professionalism.

Gender of an audience is often an issue if you are selling women's clothing, men's hats, or other items. However, when you create a brand for a man, remember that you can create ad campaigns targeting the women to purchase the products as gifts for men.

Income isn't something that many people think about when they consider an audience when developing a brand. This is often where companies go wrong. If you are selling a video gaming system that is several hundreds of dollars in a local store down the street and the average income of families in the area is less than $25,000 a year they may not be able to afford the product. You cannot sell an expensive product to a poor audience.

Also, people with a very high income may not consider purchasing a very cheap product. The value of your brand must match the income of the people you think will be your primary target as customers.

Geographical regions are also very important. Many people open businesses and try to sell products and services where there just isn't a need. This is a good way to fail. For example, if you have a company selling snow shovels then it wouldn't make sense to try to sell them to home owners in Florida. Know your geographical locations and which regions will benefit the most from your product or services.

Know Your Audience

There are many things about your audience that you must know when you are creating a brand. If you do not have a clear understanding of which your audience is then you will fail.

When you determine your audience it is important to narrow it down based on the age, gender (only if specific), geographical region (only if specific), income levels, and more. Your audience will be defined as something like 20-30 year old, male golfers that are left handed.

Some brands may not be this specific. However, the more you can narrow down your audience the more your brand will separate you from the competition. This means you will have less competition to worry about also.

Branding by Your Audience

Branding by your audience will allow you to be more successful with sales and develop long lasting customers that are dedicated to you. Targeting the wrong audience can cause problems with credibility and trust.

Older groups of people often want to see a brand as one they can trust. They want credibility and a professional look. If the image appears to be young or unprofessional then you may find that your revenues are lacking.

The same practice rings true with a younger crowd. If you are targeting a young crowd and your brand is too professional and comes across as boring then kids will not be interested in what you have to offer. For example, if your target audience is to sell super fast toy cars to five year old boys then you want a very exciting brand that is fun. If your brand is professional and so is your appearance it will be hard to convince a 5 year old that the cars are really fast.

Always brand by audience. Find out what they want to see. You may even want to talk to different age groups and find out what they would like to see. This would be a good place to start.

Your Business' Logo

Today it is common for people to say that a logo is everything when it comes to branding. This couldn't be further from the truth. A logo is important in many ways when branding but it is not where the rubber meets the road with a business and a brand. A logo is one of the smallest pieces of branding.

Business Ethics
About Logos

It is common for many companies not to have a logo at all with their company. They may just have the name of their business in bright and basic letters in front of the store. Many online site owners do the same and just write the name of the website in bold letters at the top. A logo is important for every company and a good idea to have.

A logo may be a creative way of writing your company name in bold or italic lettering, special font,, different colors, and it may even contain a picture. A good logo is the golden yellow arches in McDonalds. This is a symbol that everyone recognizes when they see the yellow arches on a highway or side street from a distance. People immediately know which restaurant the arches are for.

A logo can be just one letter or it may even be your entire name. Developing a logo may be something you put off until the end of your branding process if you are not sure what you would like it to look like.

Tips with Logos

When you do design a logo there are many things to consider so you know that you are creating a good one. These things include the colors, how busy the logo is, a tagline, memorable, and more.

Colors are very important in a logo. They can be extremely annoying if they are too bright and hard to look at and they can be too dull and boring. It is very important to choose a wise color combination with your logo. Again, consider the audience when you design the logo and choose the colors. A more professional look for an older audience should use lighter tones and pleasing colors while children enjoy primary and bright colors.

A logo should never be too busy. It should be short and sweet. You want a company logo to be simple and easy to remember. A logo that is too busy may be annoying and hard to read.

It is important to search competitor sites and verify that there are no other companies with the same name as yours with a logo that is similar. Make sure that you never copy a logo or use a logo that is almost the same as another company also. This could cause you to be in the middle of a lawsuit if you accidentally design the same thing as someone else.

Does a Logo Really Help You Sell?

There is a lot of hype about logo creation and the web is saturated with companies offering to design the perfect company logo. Logos do not help you sell products. They are not responsible for increasing revenues. No one buys a product because the logo is cool or professionally designed.

Logos do create a positive impact for a business. A company with a logo versus a company that does not have a logo looks more professional and comes across as a more credible place to shop from.

This is because a professional logo creates an image. For example, employees wearing plain blue shirts in a store do not look as professional as employees with the same plain blue shirt on and a company logo stamped on the top left chest area of the shirt.

Logos are a part of image. Your goal in branding is to create an image that has an emotional impact when the customers. This doesn't mean to add an emotional picture or throw in a tagline to make people cry.

Business Ethics

Taglines should have an impact but make a promise you are going to deliver. Pictures should not be in logos at all but if you choose to put one in a logo then make sure that it is very small and not too busy.

Chapter 5 - Business Operation

Building recognition can be a difficult task in the branding process. There are many ways that you build recognition. However, you must start from within the organization and work your way out to the customers and the competitors.

Corporate Overview

All companies need to write a brief paragraph about the company. Give an overview of the business, how you got started, and what makes you thrive today. The overview should be positive and encouraging. It should also make consumers think you are an excellent place to buy from.

Maybe you donate half of your proceed to a non-profit organization helping cancer. If so, then you would want to let people know here. A corporate overview is read often by most people when it is available. An overview should be included on websites, brochures, press releases, and more.

Business Ethics
What is Your Personality?

Your personality has a lot to do with your brand. You should make sure that your personality doesn't overpower your brand too much with the company. For example, if an advertisement or company logo would look excellent in the color yellow but you hate the color yellow then maybe you need to do a check on your personality and how it is interfering with the company brand.

It is very wise for many companies to hire a brand manager so there are not problems with personalities conflicting with a brand. The image of the company needs to be based on what looks good for the company, what is attractive to the customers, and what will sell. Your personality should not mix into the brand.

Some people say that you are your brand and your personality should shine with your brand. However, there is a fine line here with this theory. A branding manager is the best option because this person can help with image and they will have a biased point of view and they will act as a cop with the brand not allowing any personalities to interfere.

Consistency

When you are creating a brand then you need to be consistent. Consistency should take place in everything that you do. Remember, brand is your image and if you are not consistent it will not have a good impact on the consumers. The primary question that you should ask yourself is if you deliver everything you promise to your customers. The answer here should always be a yes. Delivery should be consistent at all times.

Competition

There are many things to consider about your competition when you are designing a branding campaign. Many businesses fail because they do not consider their competition. You need to do proper research about your competitors, learn what makes you different, why the customers should choose you, and much more.

Researching the Competition

You must always research your competition before you begin your brand. Every business must know who their primary competitors are. It is important to know if your company is on top of the list in the industry or exactly where you stand.

When researching competitors it is important to be thorough and learn everything about them that you can. How are you similar? Do they have the same products as you? What types of ad campaigns to they use that are successful? What campaigns to they use that are failing?

What Sets You Apart From the Competitors?

A very important factor when you are researching competitors of your products and services is that it is that you have that is different. If you have to, make a list of everything you have that they do not and vice versa. Determine what it is about your company that works.

Many the competitors left out a vital piece of information that they should be focusing on the product that they are not. This could be a perfect solution to getting a foot in and immediately ahead of the competitors.

Business Ethics

When you determine the positive aspect that is different that sets you completely apart from the competitors it may be this information used for your ad campaign.

You never want to look the same as the rest of the companies in your industry. Don't be afraid to step outside of the box and go different. This is how consumers will remember you. If you all look the same then it will be no difference to the customers when they make a choice that they are going to buy from.

Why Should Customers Shop From You?

Another part about setting yourself apart from the competitors is determining why the customers should shop from you and not the other guy. What is it about your business that makes you the right place to shop from?

If you offer sales or free shipping and the competitors don't then you should use this as a focal point right up front. If you have a product that the competitor doesn't then you should use this too. Show the customers why you are the better place. There are many ways to do this. You may have a customer service team that is available 24 hours a day and the other companies may only be open during normal business hours. This would be a focal point.

The reasons that customers should shop from you need to be clear and concise. You need to be entirely different than the rest of the businesses in your industry. Setting yourself apart from the rest is the best thing you can do because it will cause the customers to remember you specifically. There will be no confusion of which company you are in a group of businesses that look the same.

Establishing Brand

Once you have determined your mission, vision, audience, and separation from the competitors you can begin to establish your brand. There are many things that you need to do to establish your brand so people will begin to remember your name.

These things include getting inside of the customer's mind, get endorsements, find hot prospects, and use the public relations firms to your advantage. These few things will go a long way when making an effort to establish yourself amongst the competition and in the market.

Establishing a Place Inside of the Customer's Mind

One of your biggest goals in the branding process is establishing a place inside of the customer's mind. At this point, you have a good idea who your audience is supposed to be. You know what their income level is, their age, and possibly geographical details. This information is relevant in establishing an actual audience.

Your goal is to prove to the customer they have a need for your product or your service. The customer needs to find a reason why they need you. The branding techniques will tell the customer that your product resolves a problem they may have, fulfills a need they have, and makes their life much better if they purchase it. There has to be a reason to purchase the product and a positive aspect of why it is the best option to use it.

When you get inside of the customer's head the customer will believe they absolutely have to have the product. As you see many infomercials talk about how someone will become rich if they use a product or how their health will be better you need to establish the benefit of the customer so you can make them truly believe that their life will be much better when they use your product.

This also means that you have to build trust and credibility with the customers. Many products do a fantastic job of proving to the customer why a product or service is beneficial and needed. However, they fail to establish credibility or trust with the consumers. Your reputation is not at stake but it is questioned at this point so you need to provide proof that you are going to deliver the promises you are making to the customer.

Endorsements

The public and consumers listen to public figures. When you have the ability to get an endorsement on a product then you need to take advantage of it. However, you cannot wait for an endorsement to come to you. Your public relations manager may need to contact some of these figures to see if they are interested in endorsing a product. One thing to keep in mind is that endorsements may cost quite a bit of money if you are trying to get a public figure to back your product.

There are many ways to get endorsements. You may attend events where a public figure is going to be. This includes getting back stage at concerts or shows where you can have access to the person. You also can call their managers and talk to them about endorsing a product.

One thing to keep in mind about endorsements is that you need to find a figure that matches the audience also. If your target audience is teenagers then you want to find an endorsement that the teenagers know and trust. Someone that the teenagers think is hip and would want to buy the product when they find out the person uses it too. The last thing you would want to do is get an endorsement on your product by an older individual who is well known and respected by an older audience that the teenager audience has never heard of. This would be a waste of money and time on your part.

Hot Prospects

As a marketer, when branding your business or product you need to be on the lookout for hot prospects and opportunities at all times. These need to be taken advantage of when you can. It is important to use every opportunity to get your product exposure in the right methods. These methods may be trade shows or other public events.

When you attend trade shows and other events the goal is to look and be professional. If you just have a table set up with a few products on it then customers may not take you seriously. Attending events like this require professional flyers, banners, signs, and other things to get the attention of attendees. It is important to look prepared and professional.

The more events you attend the more your name gets out there. When you create banners and signs you may find a situation where someone would like to display your banner or sign. Do not charge someone for this. This is a benefit for you because it is free advertising, minus the cost of the banner. It will give you exposure and help you with the branding of your business and product.

Hot prospects need to reach out to the targeted audience for your product or service. Do not attend events that your audience is not going to be at. If there is no way that an elderly crowd will be interested in what you are offering then you are only wasting your time to make a big presentation to them at a trade show. Know

Business Ethics

who the audience is going to be at the public prospects for gaining exposure.

Using Public Relations Pros to Your Advantage

Media attention needs to be used to your advantage. There are many ways to do this. One thing to keep in mind is that your product and your brand do not have to be fully established yet to gain the attention of the media. What is important is that you use the media to help you get established.

The media can be used in many ways. Press releases are one of the best things you can do to get the exposure you are looking for and help you create a place in the industry of the business.

A press release is usually used for announcing grand openings for new businesses, new product launches, big sales and events, or anything else knew that is happening within a company.

The elements of a press release should include the event itself, why people will benefit going to it, the location, date, and time of the event. If you don't tell people where to go it will do you no good. You should also provide your company contact information in case the media wants to call you to get an interview or even write a story on the company. Customers may have questions. Without contact information it could cost you a lot of business. Also, always include your website address in a press release so people can go to your site and learn more about who you are.

Press releases are sent out to as many media outlets as you can send them to for the targeted audiences you are trying to reach out to. These media outlets include news stations, newspapers, magazines, radio stations, and more. When a media outlet receives a press release they may do a few things. They may immediately respond and use it for the next big story that hit the press and tell the public all about it. They may put it aside for when they are waiting for a slow period and then use it as a story or they will do nothing at all.

Sending out press releases doesn't cost a business anything. It is cheap and you do not need to worry about cost. It never hurts to send out press releases even if the media is not interested. The point is that you have to at least try to use public relations to your benefit. It may be that one event or announcement you have about your business that is used by the press. That one small bit of exposure could go a long way for you.

Chapter 6 - Make Your Business Known

Establishing your identity is very important when you are fighting for a place in a market or a certain niche. You may know exactly who you are but you need to get your name out there and for people to be aware of your existence also. There are many ways you can establish an identity in a local community or around the world.

Donations

Donations do you a lot of justice when it comes to establishing an identity around the local community and anywhere else. Many companies or non-profits offer plaques with your name on them, engravings in the wall, and other things when you donate money to them. This gives you exposure. When customers see your name as a company that made a donation, not only does it look good for you but it gets the company name out there permanently. This part of the branding process is important because it helps the business build credibility and trust with the customers in the market.

Investments

Investments are very important also. When you invest in a company it is important to be sure they are in the same industry as your product or service. Investing helps build a name for your company, give you more exposure and more. When you invest in a company, one of the agreements you can make when lending your money is that they provide exposure or advertising for you. Investments are very beneficial and help with the branding process.

Give Free Information

So many companies upset customers because they want to charge money for everything. This leaves a customer walking away with a bad taste in their mouth about you and only causes you to look dishonest or greedy.

There are things that you can give away for free when it comes to information. There is no way you can teach a customer everything you know in just a few minutes of talking to them or in a few pages that they can read.

Many people practice giving tips and advice through flyers and brochures. You may want to place a few useful tips on the back of your brochure. This will help build credibility and trust with customers that you are not greedy and you are willing to help them achieve certain goals. It will also prove to them that you actually

Business Ethics

have the knowledge to perform certain tasks within your company. You don't have to reveal secrets of the trade but you can give out helpful information that is useful.

Giving useful information may include offering tips and advice when you are out on a service call in a home. If your company offers plumbing services and you are on a call that the customer has frozen pipes under their home then you may recommend they leave the water dripping overnight.

This type of advice is useful to the customer and will help them not end up in a situation with a burst pipe. Although, continuous broken pipes may be a profit for you it is only one customer.

You may think it will not benefit you to tell them how to avoid problems because then they won't need you. However, there are plenty of other reasons they can call you. Plus, you will be the person they will turn to any time they need something repaired. In addition, word of mouth goes a long way with customers and the customer may attract you plenty of business your way.

Adding Value to Your Business

When you are branding it is important to add value with everything you do. Adding value means making yourself valuable to the customers and the community. This may include giving out free information through tips and tricks, statistics, and other useful bits.

You can make the business more valuable by adding a little extra in everything that you do. A voice mail message might include a quick tip on fixing something or a way to prevent a computer virus. The signature on your email should contain more than your name, address, and phone number. You might include a useful sentence underneath that is a quick tip or useful bit of information.

Making yourself useful adds value to your business and to the customers. The customers need to believe that they need you and this is a part of proving to them you are useful and the best person to turn to when they need something.

Getting Your Brand Out There

So you have designed a logo, a name, a tagline, and anything else. Now you need to practice other methods to get your name all over the place. This can be done with clothing, pens, cups, and other paraphernalia.

Clothing is one of the best things you can get out there on people. If you design t-shirts with your company name and logo on them people will wear them. These should be free items that you give away to people as they visit your booth, table, or even take a survey. You may offer the t-shirts to people if they give you feedback on their opinions for certain things. They may provide their information or email which also is a contact you just made.

Always hold onto this information as you can use it in an email campaign. One thing to consider is that when you ask customers for an email address, always ask them if it is okay to contact them via email. Do not assume that it is okay or you may upset them. One thing that is okay is sending a flyer, brochure, or coupon in the regular snail mail.

Clothing works in many ways. People wear free t-shirts all over the world. They may travel to different destinations like a gym working out, a beach, or a fair. This is exposure for you for every person that sees this person. The more t-shirts you get out there the better for your business.

Business Ethics

One thing to keep in mind with printed materials as advertising techniques to spread the company name is that you want to create things that are useful for people. A pen with your company name is more useful than a koozie. Pens will never be thrown away because someone will use them until the ink runs out.

They are very cheap to make and easy to distribute. You can give a package of pens to a business that you know spends a lot of time traveling around the world. Before you know it your pens were left in meetings and other places and now you have people checking out your site from other countries. It is as easy as that when you distribute items with your company name on them.

You have to get your name out there and create your popularity. You can do this by designing t-shirts and other useful things for the business. Try to give these things away for free so you can have the best results with your branding. Also, make sure that the items created look nice and represent your brand as you want to be portrayed. Match the scheme.

Get One on One with the Customers

Getting one on one with the customers is very important. You need to talk to the customers and let them know that you are there for them if they have questions and that you really exist. Companies need representatives of a business so they are existent. It is hard for a business to gain exposure when they don't have someone to actually talk to.

If your business targets a local community then it is important to get out there and talk to the community. Remember you are looking for the audience who is going to benefit from your product. These are the people you want to talk to.

If you have a business on the web then you will need to get one on one with the customers by providing access to a direct chat option. This gives customers a good feeling but they know that someone really exists. When you offer a direct chat they have the ability to contact a live person rather than talk to a machine. Customers despise machines, automated phone systems, and more. They will try to avoid them and it can give them a bad taste in their mouth about the business. Try to be as responsive as possible with the customers.

Local Business Events

Other local business events are extremely important. Not only do you want to target your local or national audience but you also want to attend other business events. You may find a company struggling that may need your assistance. You might find a company that you can work with together on a project in trade for advertising or even help you build your credibility.

Business Ethics

Local business events help you network in the big industry that you may be working in. It is important to talk to companies and let them know you are out there. Maybe you will recommend one company while they recommend you. Always talk to other businesses, let them know about who you are and what you are all about, what their benefit is by knowing you, and how you can help each other. Give them something to remember you by and make an impact.

When you attend events and network with other companies and people then you provide another form of advertising. Networking works very well because when someone does come across a situation where they could use your product or service they will remember you. Creating contacts is a very big part of branding. It also helps instill your company name in the minds of people around the industry.

Media Consideration

Media is extremely important when branding a business. There are many different outlets and they can be used in many different ways to your advantage and even for damage control. Proper branding means staying tight with the media as your friend. Some say to keep your friends close and your enemies closer and this is true with the media. They can make you very popular or ruin you but nothing really in between. You need the media on your side at all times.

Local Media

There are many different local media outlets that you might consider using when you are looking to brand your company or a product. You can use local newspapers to announce sales, events, and other things. The television stations are useful when running advertisements or events on the news.

One thing to keep in mind is that public television stations are free and they cannot charge you money to run something on them. If you are a non-profit organization looking to brand your organization the best way to do it is through public television stations. You can announce events like blood drives and other things on public television. This is great exposure and it is free.

Other methods of local media may be local websites for town members. Some towns have a site for the community where people can post things like classified ads and other things. They are free sites and sometimes used more than the newspapers because of this.

Article Writing for Press

Another way you can use the media to your advantage is to write your own articles and distribute them to the press. This is very beneficial. If the press comes across times they need to fill additional space in their paper they may use them.

Sending articles to the press is free. The will not charge you to use them. If you write beneficial articles to magazines in the industry you work in then you may even get paid for the article.

Business Ethics

Article writing is a very beneficial way to advertise your business and helps with the branding process.

Sponsors

Looking for sponsors is very important. It is very similar to getting an endorsement. You may make a deal with companies to sponsor you that might include putting up an advertisement at a local event or charity you are holding. Sponsors need to see a benefit in it for them and they are usually willing. When you find local sponsors it helps build credibility with your business. You should always look for local or national sponsors.

Sponsors can be used on your website and at your local business. The most common way to obtain a sponsor is by offering them advertising for their business.

Written Testimonials

Written testimonials are very important in the branding process because they work in two ways. They help build credibility and trust with the targeted audience.

When you sell products or services to customers it is important to gather as many written testimonials that you can from customers. A customer can write up the type of product or service they purchased from your company and their experience working with you. The more written testimonials you have the better.

Written testimonials are beneficial because they create hype. They increase the excitement about your business and make people want to try your product. Testimonials tell the public that you followed through on delivering the promise made. This means that consistency is present and it is very important.

Without written testimonials it is hard to prove that you deliver. It is hard to build a brand without people to back you like endorsements through public figures and people in the community.

Special Offers

Building a brand also requires you to provide offers and special discounts to the customers. Customers are always looking for a great deal and when they know they can get it from you they will shop from you.

You might offer discount codes to customers for specific items or even a buy one get one free deal. These are excellent ways to promote a business. If you have an online company then you may offer free shipping or other types of discounts to people during a specified period of time.

Special offers work very well with customers. Free items usually work the best because customers find that nothing is ever free. Although it is not cost effective to give away free items you may include something free with a purchase of a bigger item.

Referrals

Another media consideration when you are building up your brand is that you need to work on referrals. Referrals work very well in building up your brand. This is word of mouth through customers who swear by you. These can be difficult to build up but when you get referrals it helps with credibility.

You can help with gaining referrals to your business by offering specials or discounts to customers that refer you to other customers. This may be a $5 discount on their next purchase or something else. When the customer sees there is a benefit in it for them they will often times refer the company to gain the benefit. This helps increase a customer base, revenues, and build up your brand.

Inserts

Inserts are very beneficial to brand building and a perfect use of the media. Some newspapers or brochures may have a cost associated with adding an insert in a newspaper while others may allow you to provide an insert for free.

Inserts in newspapers and magazines allow for more exposure of the company. Even if a customer doesn't thoroughly read an insert they will remember the name of the company and your logo. It creates a stamp in their mind about you and the products and services offered. This way if they come across a situation where they need a product or your service they will think of the business. Inserts work well and are very beneficial for getting into the mind of customers.

The Competitive Edge

Creating a competitive edge is another important aspect of branding. Today, the online world has many methods of branding. The most popular method of branding and gaining the competitive edge is through the use of Blogs. Blogs allow a site to increase traffic, improve rank through search engine results, and even helps with credibility building also.

About Blogs

Blogs are websites that use the new Web 2.0 technology which allows visitors to a site to post their own comments, articles, and more. Giving a user the access to post things to your site allows them to feel a sense of ownership to the business. They work in many ways which may include forums, discussion boards, or even look like a daily diary in a sense. They keep the visitors up to date on current events and allow for discussion to take place.

Reasons to Use Blogs

There are many reasons to use blogs for a business. A business may want to provide a discussion board that allows other customers to discuss troubleshooting tips and tricks. A company may post useful information about how to get the most longevity out of products, how to repair or fix things, and even how to prevent problems from occurring.

Using a Blog to Your Benefit

If you do decide to add a blog to your company site then there are many things to consider so you get the most out of it. Some companies allow people to post their own content while others cannot. Consider things like keywords and phrases, links, useful information, and even contact information.

The primary purpose of blog writing for branding is to gain more exposure to a business and get the word out to people that the company exists. Blogs are an excellent way to create hype and exposure because the web has millions of businesses and customers.

Business Ethics

When using a blog it is important to make sure that you use important keywords that are relevant to the products and services offered by your business.

These keywords and phrases should be the words that will be typed into the search engines when a user is looking for what you offer. The keywords should be used naturally throughout the content of the blog. They will work by allowing your blog to be pulled up in the search engine results when users type in the specific keywords and phrases you used in the blog.

Adding links to blogs is a very important thing for two reasons. They provide an easy method to get back to your site and provide an inbound link. Users always appreciate an easy way to get to your company. If you are talking about products and services offered in a blog without links to where the customers can find them then it will do no good.

Customers will only search for a business for a very short period if they search at all. You have a better chance of a customer when a link is right there in the blog so they can easily click and find out more about the company.

URLs are also beneficial for a business because they provide inbound links. One of the ways that search engines work is that one of the ways they rank a business is through popularity. Popularity can be built up by links integrated within blogs. The more inbound links you provide inside of a blog the more popularity a search engine thinks you have. Never forget to place inbound links inside of blogs and content you place on your blog.

A blog needs to provide beneficial information for the visitors and readers. When there is something useful to the reader they will come back for more. Blogs give you the opportunity to give the free advice and useful information that will benefit the users and cause you to gain credibility for being knowledgeable about the products and services offered.

Reinforcement of Your Brand

The most important thing about branding is that you need to constantly reinforce the promises you make to the targeted audience. A branding program can be reinforced by being consistent.

Consistency is the most important factor when you reinforce. It shows that you are serious about your brand and your product. It is important to be consistent to show credibility with the customers and the public eye. When a company is not consistent it looks bad for a company as if they are disorganized or have problems.

Reinforcing your brand needs to be done on a regular basis. You should practice constant branding techniques that work for your company.

Schedule them weekly or monthly if you have to. For example, try to send out at least two press releases a month to numerous media contacts. Let them know how you are doing and what is going on with the company. Make announcements about ways you better the community and people who use your products.

Reinforcement works for a business with the media also. When you are continuously in contact with the media it will benefit you when something bad happens. Having the media on your side is very important. They will help you with damage control when a customer makes an accusation or if you need assistance with a bad situation.

Business Ethics

Reinforcing your brand means that you back what you say you are going to do. You need to prove to the customers that what you say you will do is true and continuously reinforcing this will brand the idea into their minds.

Branding is something that every business needs to practice on a daily basis or whenever the opportunity arises. You must work hard to ensure that you make an impact on the way customers think about the products or services offered to the communities.

When you practice branding you need to ensure you are targeting the right audience demographics. Logos are important but they are not your selling point. They just make a statement. Use a tagline along with a logo or with an advertisement only when you think it will grab the attention of customers in a positive way.

Branding requires you to use media outlets to your benefit. You must be proactive in your methods of branding. You can hire someone to do the branding for you. A business has complete control over their brand and their image. The goal of branding is to get into the minds of customers in a positive way and help them realize your business offers a beneficial product to them. You have something that they need.

Branding requires you to separate yourself from the competition proving why the business is the best option to purchase from. There needs to be a clear picture what makes you different, unique, and why a customer should choose you over the competition.

The thing to remember about branding is that it helps produce an image about a business. Consistency is very important. You cannot perform branding by creating a logo on a website and walking away. Branding requires proactive approaches of exposure through article writing, press release distribution, public appearances, products with logos, and much more. Trust and credibility must be built through the branding process. By using these techniques you can be off to an amazing start of building a trustworthy brand that customers can rely on.

Also, always follow through with promises you make to customers through a mission or any statements.

Chapter 7 - Negotiation Mastery

To really understand this first you need to look at what the word 'negotiation' means. The definition of the word 'negotiation' is a dialogue between two or more people or parties who wish to; resolve a difference of opinion, reach a mutual understanding, agree upon a course of action and to bargain for an advantage. Basically you are looking for ways to settle your differences.

The reason you want to negotiate with someone is so that both parties can find a suitable solution. Otherwise disputes and arguments may arise that can harm relationships permanently.

Neither person is going to be in charge of the negotiation. You must be prepared to discuss your differences no matter what they are, and then find a common ground.

The best way to negotiate is to prepare for it in advance. This way you are going to get a much better outcome. If you start negotiating on the spot you are more likely to run into issues and ending up arguing more than negotiating.

Michael Hendricks

While you may tend to think of negotiation skills when it comes to businesses and corporations. You do, in fact, negotiate on a regular basis. Have you ever tried to haggle for a better price on a product? This is negotiating. When you buy a new vehicle you are expected to negotiate on the price.

Even small children try to negotiate on things like bed time, going to a friend's house and when to get their chores done. This type of negotiating is done on the spur of the moment in an attempt to stall for time or to put off doing something.

Quite often you may be prepared to negotiate for a lengthy time period and are shocked when your terms are agreed upon almost immediately. It never hurts to try and negotiate for something, you don't know all the details of what the other person is thinking.

In certain situations it takes confidence to negotiate for something. Whether it is a better rate on a hotel booking or a discount on a new fridge or freezer.

Of course you can tempt the situation by suggesting that you are more likely to become a repeat buyer when you are offered a great price. So never be afraid to ask for a better deal, you may just get what you ask for in return.

Once you begin negotiating you may find it very exciting and when you get results you may be ready to negotiate more often.

Business Ethics
The Basic Skills Needed

If you want to improve your negotiation skills then there are a few basic things that you will need to learn. Successful negotiators are those that have the skills necessary to make things happen the way they want them to. This is done with ethics and by having a personable personality.

One of the most basic skills you need for negotiating is that you need to have a plan in mind before the negotiation starts. As with any type of meeting it always pays to be well prepared in advance. If you do not have a plan in mind then it is very possible that things will backfire on you, and you won't get the deal that you had hoped for. Make sure you know what the other party is looking for and what their priorities are.

Ensure that you know who you will be dealing with. If you are going into a business negotiation research them and find out who they are and what their future plans are. This way you can address any issues that might come up during your negotiation.

Different types of people can be dealt with best by responding in various ways. This could be answering objections and concerns with solid statistical information. Some people are looking for tons of information while others are content with just a basic overview. Yet again others may want to see facts and figures in the form of slides, diagrams and detailed graphics.

When you know who you are dealing with, it will be easier to respond with them to achieve your own desired results.

Another huge asset of skill of a negotiator is the art of knowing how to listen. Even before you start negotiating ask questions to try and find out what the other party is hoping to achieve. People love to talk so give them the opportunity and then pay attention to what they have to say. This is a great way to attain leverage.

Good negotiators are confident people and this applies to both how you conduct your meetings and to your body language. Always ensure that you are mentally prepared for your meeting, if not the other party may pick up on this and try and use it against you.

Another important skill set to have is to not be a salesperson. Instead you must acknowledge that both parties are needed to get this deal achieved. Your goal is not to be the overpowering party, instead you want to be seen as the person who helps come to a mutual understanding. Be the person in control!

Negotiation and Reputation

Negotiation is a two sided event, if you want to be known as a good negotiator then you have to build a reputation for this. As with any reputation you have to allow others to trust you. This cannot be done successfully if you negotiate by using cheap tricks and bad business ethics. So how do you build a good reputation for negotiation?

The key to this is to understand what trust is all about. We have all met people that we trust along with those that we don't. The key factor to remember here is that you are negotiating with or on behalf of someone. After all negotiating is all about reaching a common and satisfactory solution for all parties.

It is going to be very difficult to reach a deal or solution with someone you ultimately don't trust. You won't ever be happy with anything they suggest. Both negotiators need to be able to trust each other, this is basically the only way a good deal will be struck.

Business Ethics

Once a deal is done everyone involved has to know and trust that the other party will deliver. There is no point going through a ton of agony or heartache wondering if the other side is going to come through for you.

Good negotiators will learn to know how to create trust during their meeting or discussion. Of course, tricky and difficult points are going to come up, this is why there is a need for negotiations in the first place.

It is important to remember here that trusting and agreeing are not the same thing. You don't have to agree with the other side, but you do need to trust them!

Always remember that during any negotiation both parties want to feel as though they have the upper hand. Of course this includes not doing anything illegal or unethical.

Your main concern right now is to build your reputation as a negotiator and this means getting the other party to trust you. Once they trust you it will be much easier for you both to reach a deal or solution.

All the actions that you take during this time are going to help set your platform for your next negotiation. If your reputation isn't build on trust then it just makes your job harder.

As you successfully conclude negotiations your reputation will follow you and before you know it you will be an in demand negotiator.

Michael Hendricks

Negotiation vs. Desperation

The worst thing anyone can do is to start negotiating with someone because you are desperate. Desperation is something that a skilled negotiator will look for and then take advantage of.

The minute you show to someone that you are desperate your power of negotiation has just been compromised. You automatically start to think in a different way and pass power to your opponent.

One skill that a good negotiator has is the ability to research their opponent. This is why it is so important for you to know who you will be negotiating with.

Many business owners will study the stock market for trading information on a particular company before starting any type of negotiations with them.

They may discover they are losing money or that they are in the middle of buying out another company. All of this information can come in very handy during any negotiation.

You can avoid looking desperate by carefully preparing questions in advance. This can help you stay on topic no matter which direction your discussion is headed. Try to put yourself in the shoes of the other party, what type of questions would you be asking them. Then try and prepare answers so you won't be taken off guard.

If your situation is truly desperate then our best advice to you is to have another person with you while the negotiations are occurring. This might be a lawyer, family member, your manager or someone else that you trust, plus someone that can give you helpful advice as necessary.

Business Ethics

Remember you never have to be alone when negotiating. Even if your voice will make the final decision, it never hurts to be backed up by a team of advisors or supporters.

The worst thing anyone can do, who even feels slightly desperate, is to act too quickly. Don't rush or allow yourself to be rushed into making any type of decision. If you feel that the other party is rushing you, take this as a signal that they may be hiding something. Never sign on that dotted line too quickly.

If time is going on and no deal is in site then it doesn't hurt to ask for more time to negotiate things further the following day or week. If your situation is getting tense this is the perfect way to diffuse it, by asking for more time to reach a decision.

When you are feeling desperate your emotions can often get in the way. Try to keep everything separate while the negotiation is being conducted. If possible keep your feelings well hidden.

Basic Negotiation Tips

1. Look for some type of common ground when you first begin your negotiation. You are building up rapport and spending time just getting to know the other person or party involved.

2. Look and identify who the main players are - always watch to see who is in charge. This will be the person that others will look to when it comes to making a final decision. This might be a manager or CEO or it could be the medical secretary that has the power to offer you a discount on your bill.

3. React surprised when an offer is made - this may take a little practice to achieve. By acting surprised you can make the other

party feel a little uncomfortable. Your goal here is to indicate that you were looking for something totally different.

4. If you can't bring yourself to ask outright for a discount, use the terms 'more affordable option' instead. This can be applied to products or when hiring some type of service provider. Just by asking what other options are available can easily get you a better deal or better value for your money.

5. When you feel as though your negotiations aren't going anywhere or taking too long, it is time to simply ask for your discount or deal. Many times this will get things resolved quickly and to everyone's satisfaction. Stop talking and ask!

6. Offering to pay for a service in full can often allow you to jump ahead in the line. You can turn this around as well. If you are the service provider say to your customer that you will get the job done within x number of hours if they pay upfront. Can be a great tactic to use if you happen to have a slow period.

7. Instead of asking for a discount try to use different wording instead. Many places today offer discounts for members of the military. So instead of asking do you etc, you ask what is your discount for military members?

8. Always get quotes and offers in writing. Just because your dentist offers to give you a discount on your next visit, ask them to give you a note that says this. They are extremely busy and it is easy for them to forget what they have said and to whom.

9. Spend time browsing in the store before asking for your discount. The minute you show a sales clerk that you are interested in one of their products, you have become more valuable to them. By taking the time to browse around and ask questions you are

Business Ethics

more likely to be offered a discount. You've stayed this long and the store wants your cash before you leave.

10. Paying in cash is another good way to get a deal or bargain. Especially in some of the smaller stores. Having the ability to pay electronically is great but the software needed is expensive. Then on top of this there are costs per transactions. The store owner is often happy to give you a discount for a cash purchase, as they still come out ahead.

About The Author

Michael Hendricks' forte is teaching professionals in different industries and disciplines how to master practical business knowledge and skills. Michael has several years of experience in leading a multimillion-dollar marketing and Communication Company that now serves many of the most notable businesses.

Michael Hendricks believes that he can help more by writing this book. He is married and lives New Jersey.